Acknowledgements

The publishers would like to thank the following for permission to reproduce photographs :

Mike Dudley (with permission of NES Arnold) : 9
NRSC Ltd / Science Photo Library : 26
Tom Van Sant / Geosphere Project, Santa Monica, Science Photo Library : 4, 5, 6, 7.

Oxford New York
Athens Auckland Bangkok Bogota Bombay
Buenos Aires Calcutta Cape Town Dar es Salaam
Delhi Florence Hong Kong Istanbul Karachi
Kuala Lumpur Madras Madrid Melbourne
Mexico City Nairobi Paris Singapore
Taipei Tokyo Toronto

and associated companies in
Berlin Ibadan

Oxford is a trade mark of Oxford University Press

ISBN 0 19 831 840 5

My Very First

OXFORD ATLAS

Editorial Adviser

Patrick Wiegand

Oxford University Press

Contents

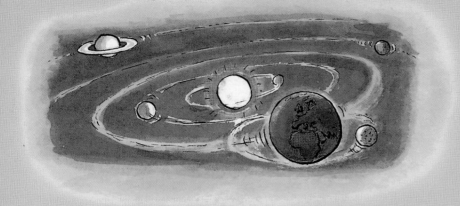

The Earth

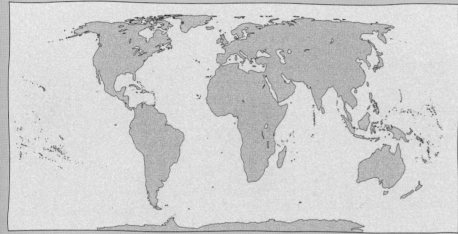

Maps of the World

Maps of Europe

A list of the maps in this atlas.

British Isles

Maps of the British Isles

Index   page 32

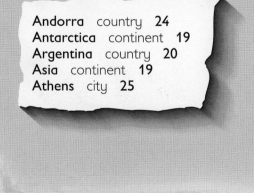

4 This is the Earth in space.

6   The Earth is round, like a ball.

8   There is land and sea.

A globe is a model of the Earth.

10   Each view of the Earth is different.

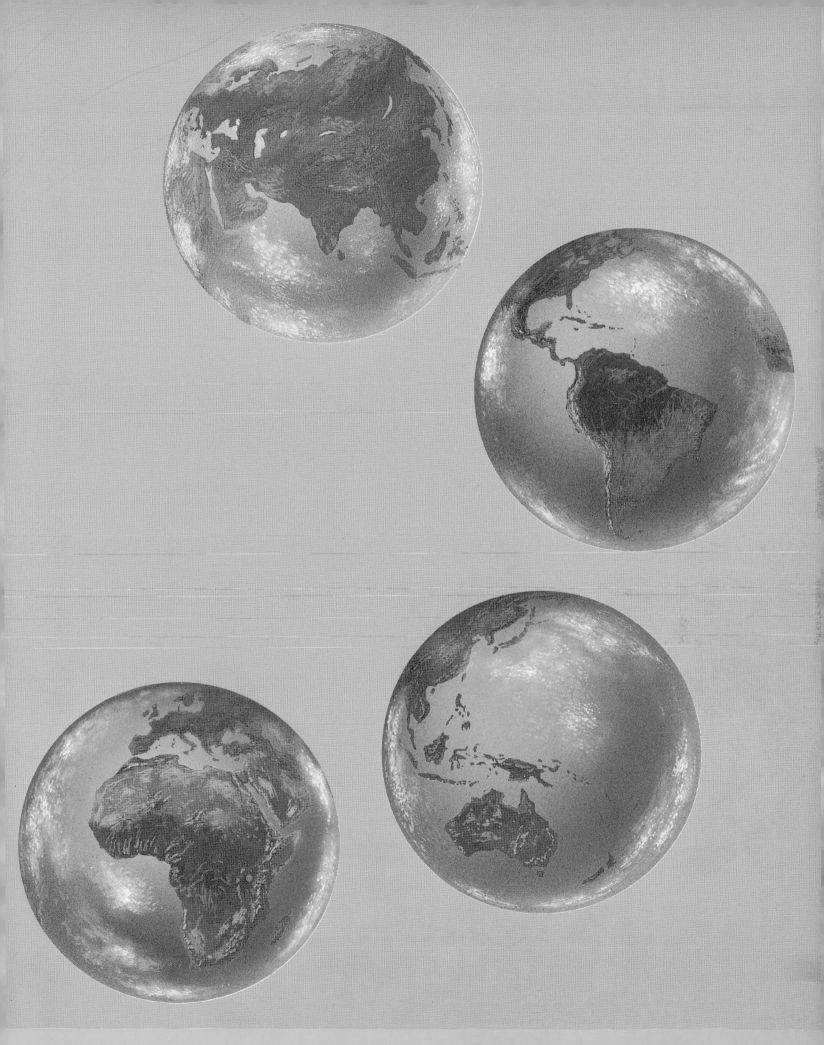

The World

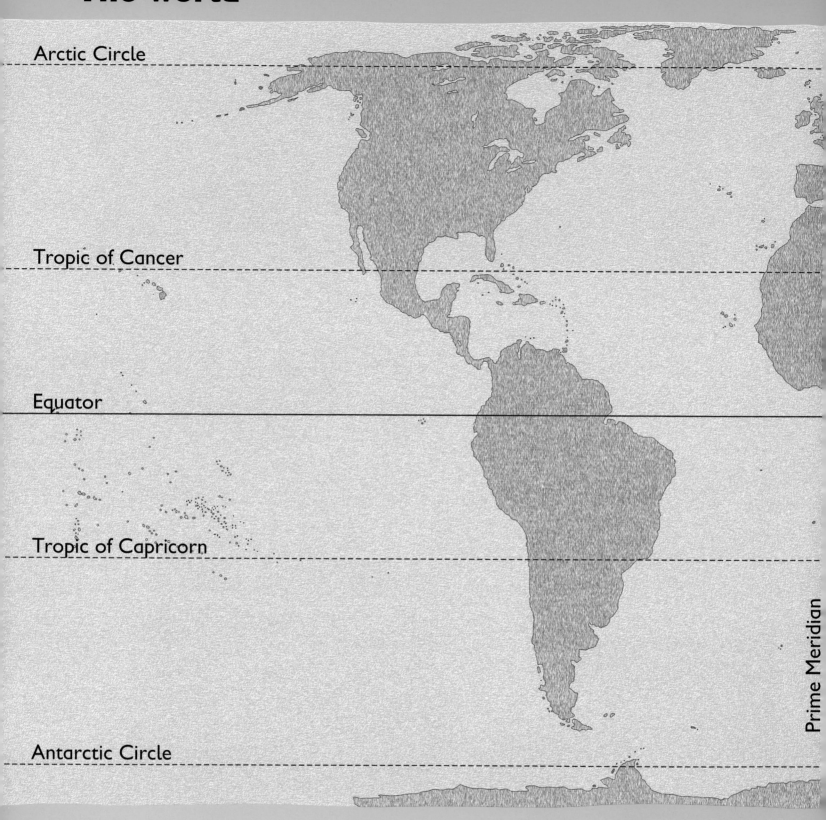

Arctic Circle

Tropic of Cancer

Equator

Tropic of Capricorn

Antarctic Circle

Prime Meridian

This is a map of the World.

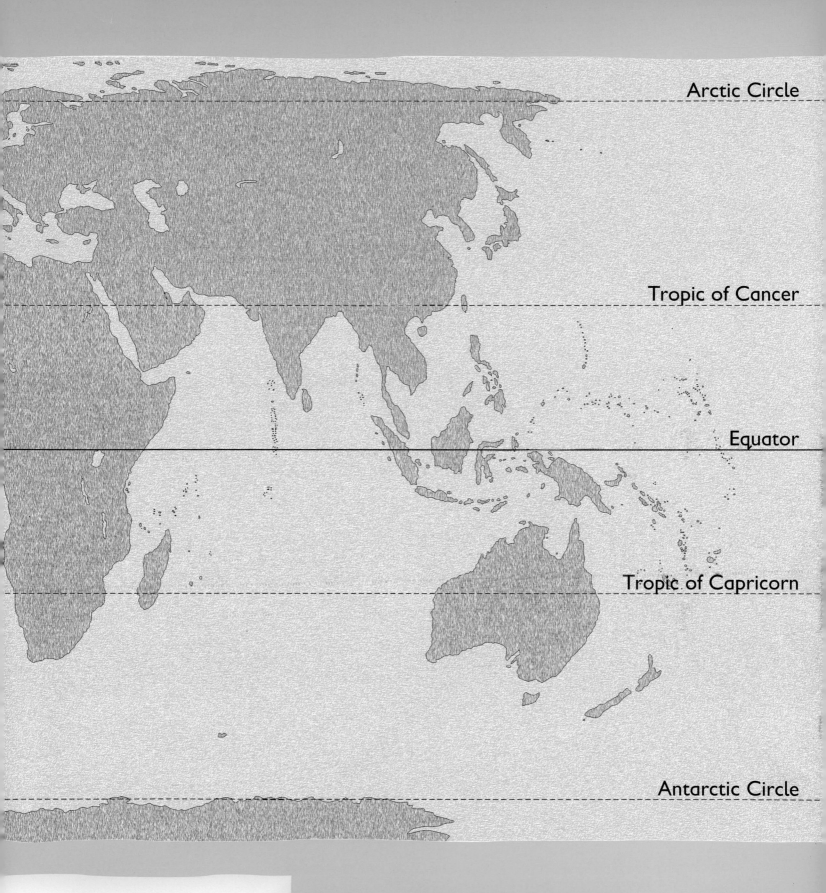

Arctic Circle

Tropic of Cancer

Equator

Tropic of Capricorn

Antarctic Circle

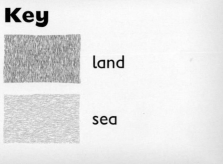

Key

land

sea

The World

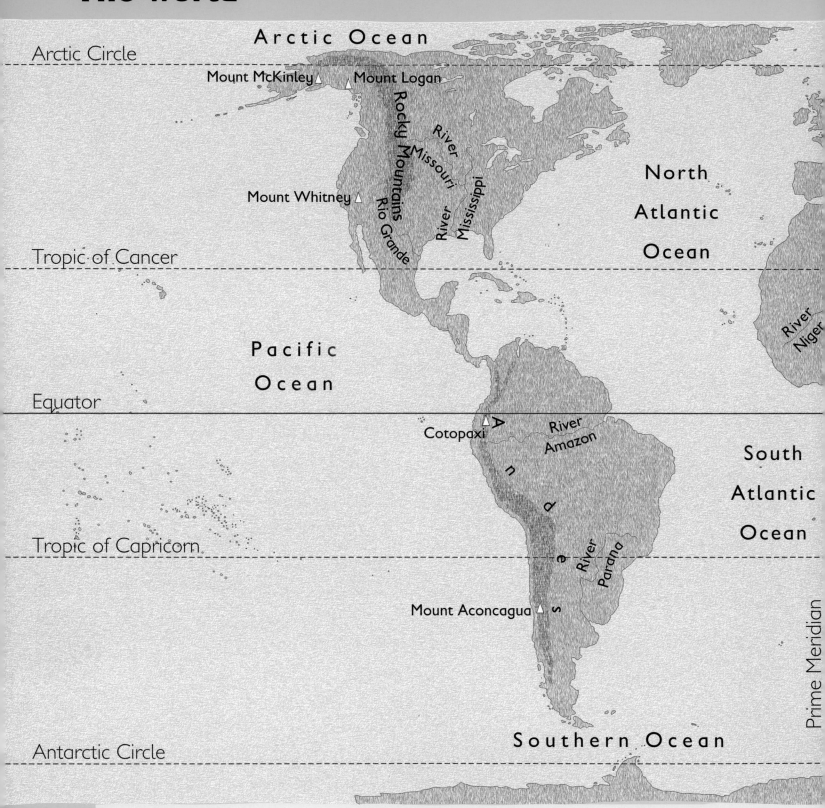

Arctic Ocean

Arctic Circle

Mount McKinley △   △ Mount Logan

Rocky Mountains

River Missouri

River Mississippi

Mount Whitney △

Rio Grande

North Atlantic Ocean

Tropic of Cancer

Pacific Ocean

River Niger

Cotopaxi △ A

River Amazon

Equator

n

South Atlantic Ocean

d

Tropic of Capricorn

e

River Parana

Mount Aconcagua △ s

Prime Meridian

Southern Ocean

Antarctic Circle

14   There are rivers and mountains.

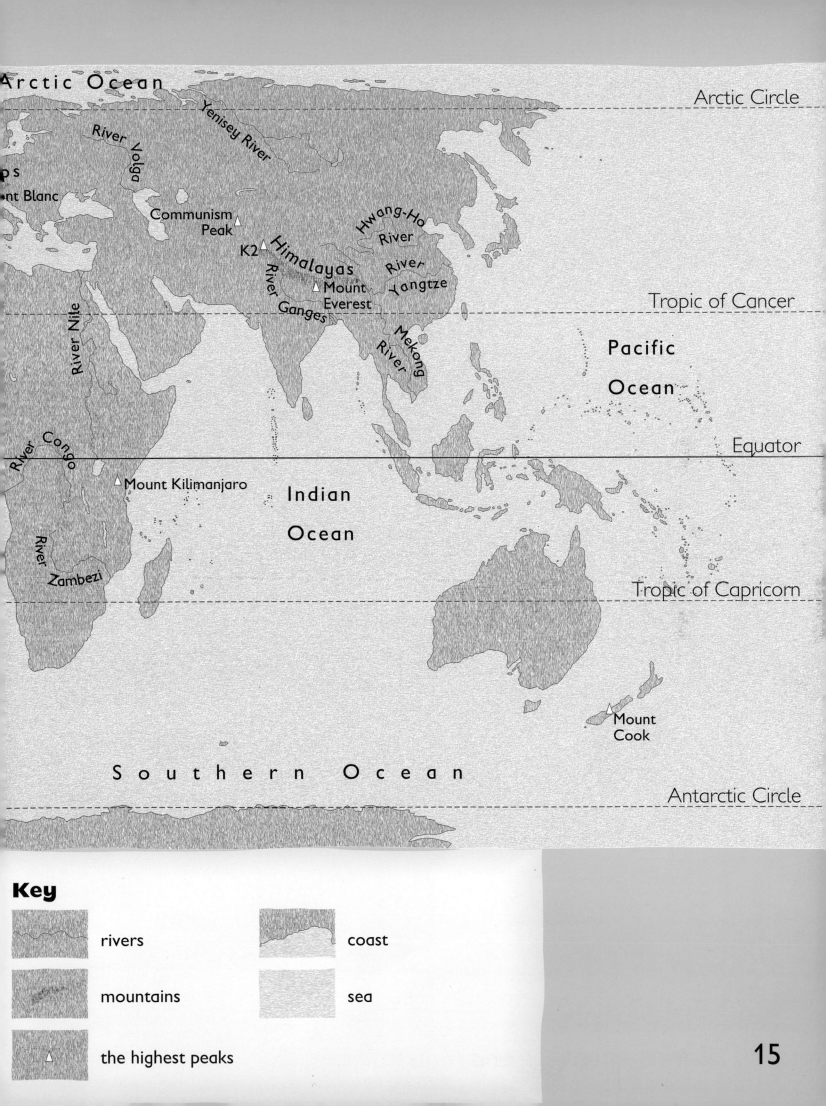

Arctic Ocean

Yenisey River

River Volga

ps

nt Blanc

Communism
Peak △

K2 △   Himalayas

River
Ganges

△ Mount
Everest

Hwang-Ho
River

River
Yangtze

Tropic of Cancer

Mekong
River

Pacific

Ocean

River Nile

Equator

River Congo

△ Mount Kilimanjaro

Indian

Ocean

River
Zambezi

Tropic of Capricorn

△ Mount
Cook

S o u t h e r n   O c e a n

Antarctic Circle

Key

	rivers		coast
	mountains		sea
△	the highest peaks		

The World

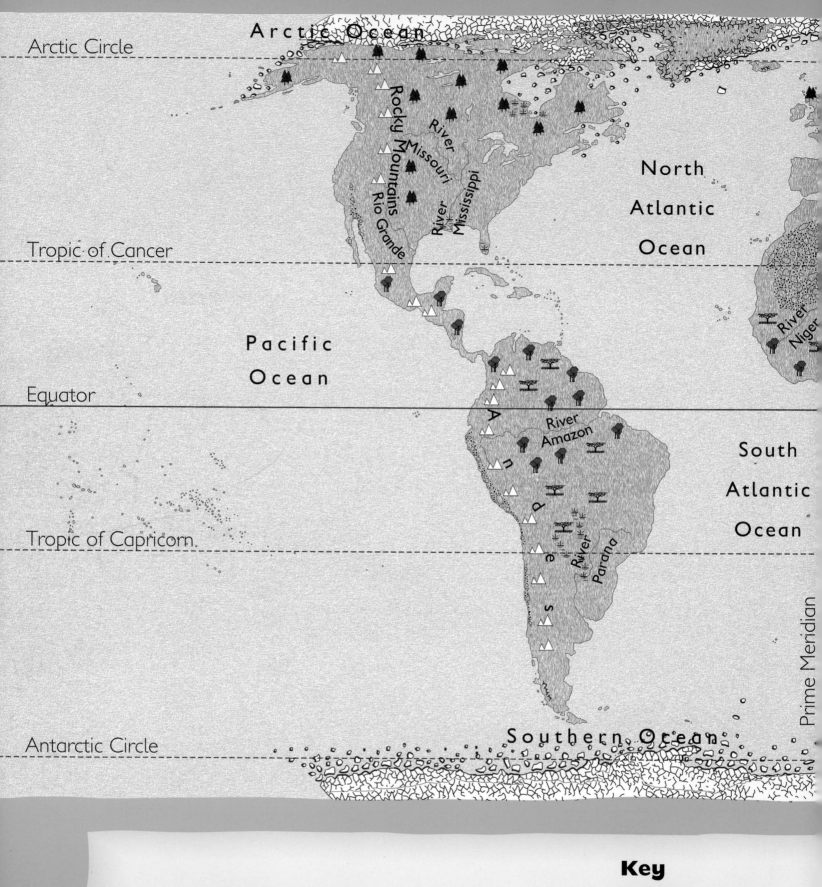

Arctic Circle

Arctic Ocean

Rocky Mountains

River Missouri

River Mississippi

Rio Grande

North

Atlantic

Ocean

Tropic of Cancer

Pacific

Ocean

Equator

A
n
d
e
s

River
Amazon

River
Parana

South

Atlantic

Ocean

River Niger

Tropic of Capricorn

Prime Meridian

Antarctic Circle

Southern Ocean

Key

 rivers

 mountains

Environments.

Arctic Ocean

Arctic Circle

River Volga

Yenisey River

Hwang-Ho River

Himalayas

River Yangtze

River Ganges

Mekong River

Tropic of Cancer

Pacific Ocean

ahara

River Nile

Equator

River Congo

Indian Ocean

River Zambezi

Tropic of Capricorn

S o u t h e r n   O c e a n

Antarctic Circle

Key

cold forest	savannah	marsh
desert	hot forest	ice

The World

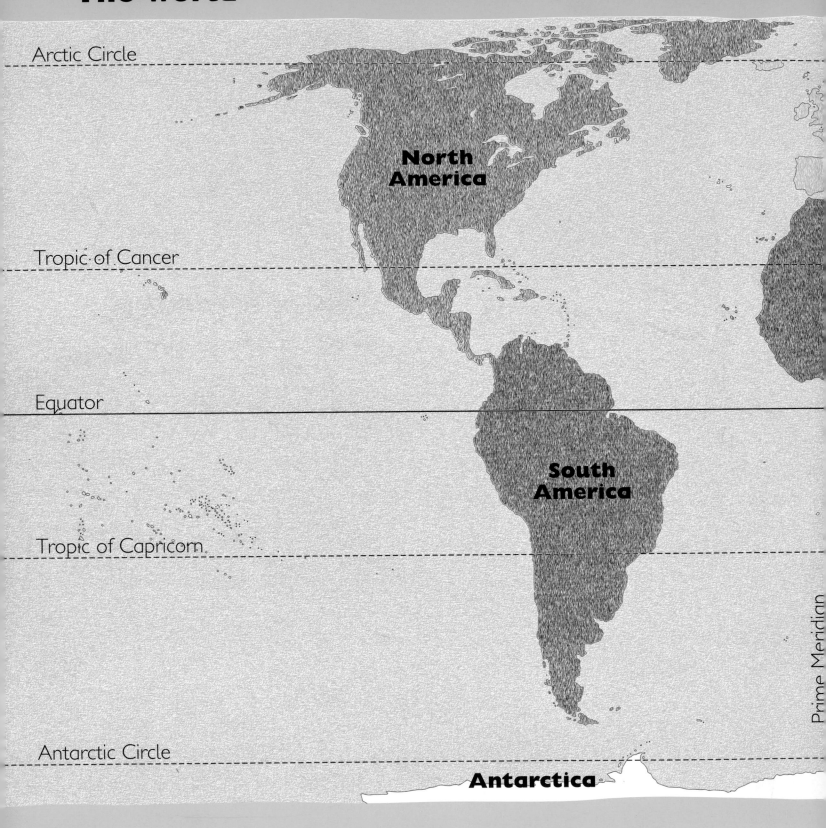

Arctic Circle

North America

Tropic of Cancer

Equator

South America

Tropic of Capricorn

Prime Meridian

Antarctic Circle

Antarctica

Key

These colours are used to show where one continent ends and another begins.

There are seven continents.

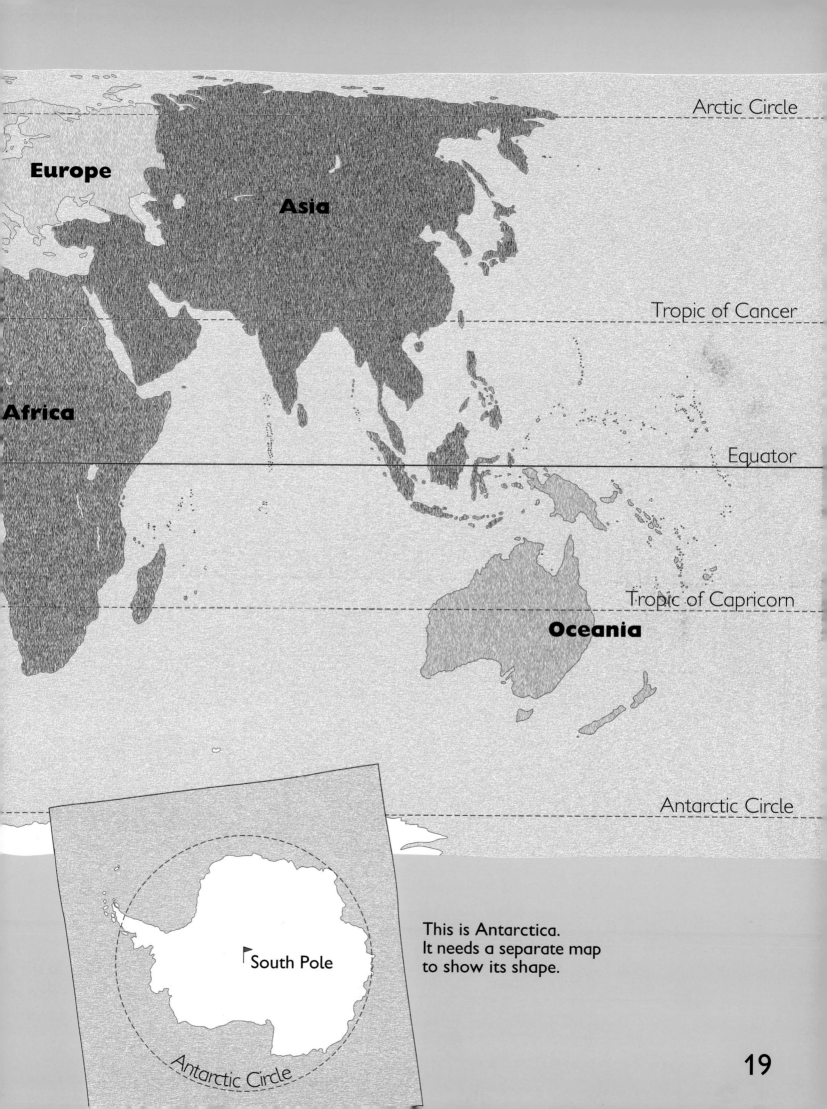

Arctic Circle

Europe

Asia

Tropic of Cancer

Africa

Equator

Tropic of Capricorn

Oceania

Antarctic Circle

South Pole

This is Antarctica.
It needs a separate map
to show its shape.

Antarctic Circle

19

The World

Arctic Circle

Canada

United Kingdom

London
Par
France

United States
of America

New York

Los Angeles

Algeria

Tropic of Cancer

Mexico

Jamaica

Mexico City

Barbados

Trinidad
and Tobago

Venezuela

Equator

Brazil

Tropic of Capricorn

Sao Paulo

Buenos Aires

Argentina

Prime Meridian

Antarctic Circle

Countries and some major cities.

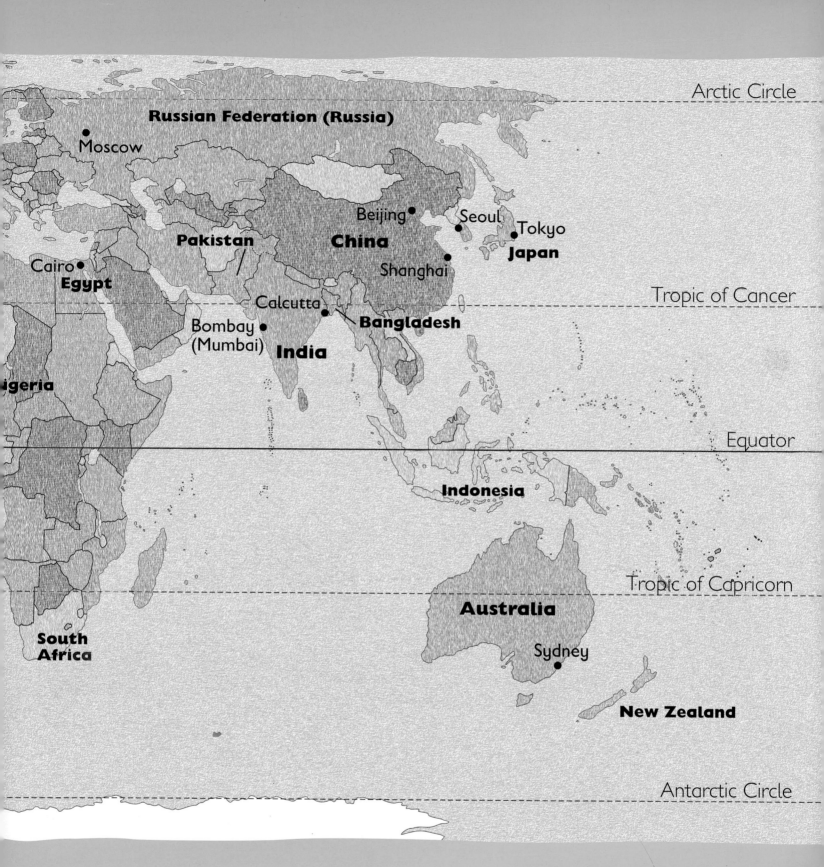

Arctic Circle

Russian Federation (Russia)

Moscow •

Beijing • Seoul
China • Tokyo
Pakistan **Japan**
Cairo • Shanghai •
Egypt

Tropic of Cancer

Calcutta •
Bombay •
(Mumbai) **Bangladesh**
India

igeria

Equator

Indonesia

Tropic of Capricorn

Australia

**South
Africa**

Sydney •

New Zealand

Antarctic Circle

Key

These colours are used to show where
one country ends and another begins.
Some countries are named on the map.

• major cities

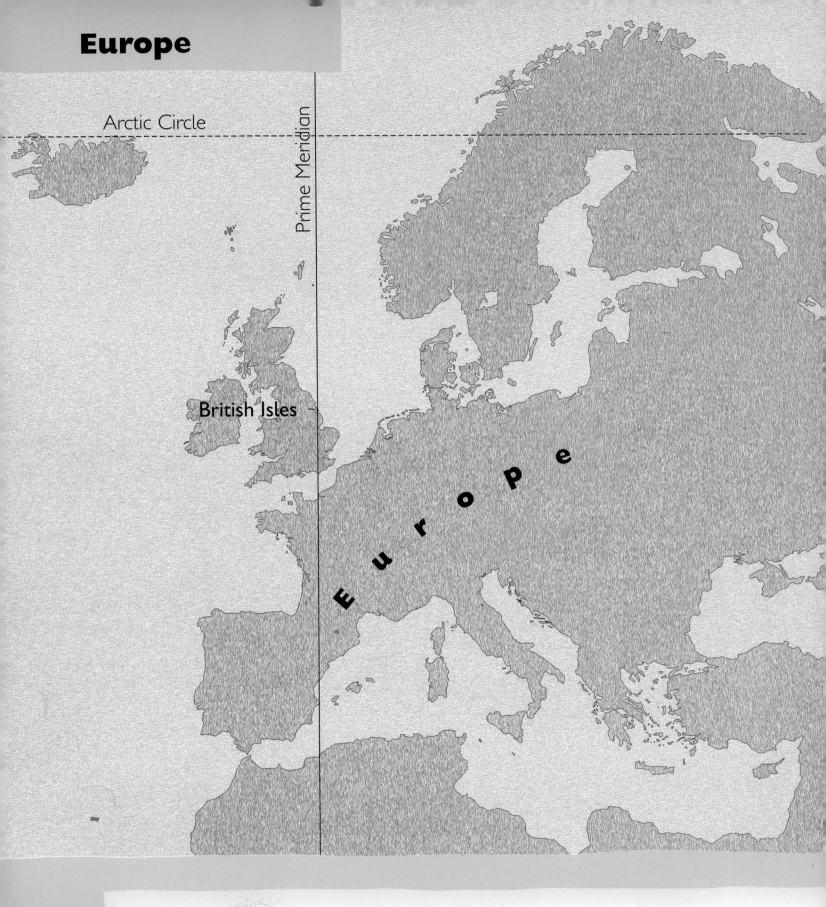

Arctic Circle

Prime Meridian

British Isles

Europe

Europe is the smallest continent.

Key

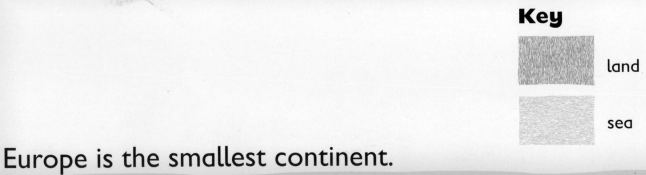

land

sea

Europe

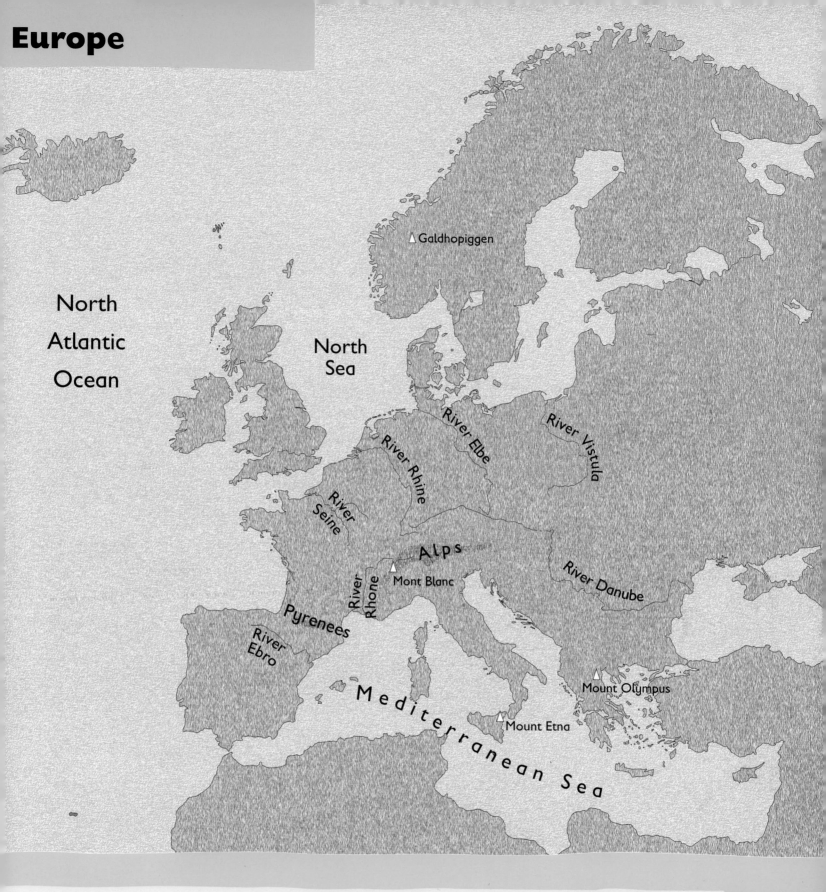

North
Atlantic
Ocean

North
Sea

△ Galdhopiggen

River Elbe

River Vistula

River Rhine

River
Seine

Alps

River
Rhone

△ Mont Blanc

River Danube

Pyrenees

River
Ebro

Mount Olympus △

△ Mount Etna

M e d i t e r r a n e a n   S e a

Rivers and mountains.

Europe

Iceland

Norway

Sweden

Finland

Estonia

Russian Federatio (Russia)

Latvia

Lithuania

Denmark

United Kingdom

Republic of Ireland

Belarus

Netherlands

Poland

Germany

Czech Republic

Ukraine

Belgium

Luxembourg

Liechtenstein

Slovakia

Switzerland

Austria

Hungary

Moldova

France

Slovenia

Croatia

Romania

Yugoslavia

Monaco

San Marino

Bulgaria

Andorra

Bosnia-Herzegovina

Italy

FYRO Macedonia

Portugal

Spain

Albania

Turkey

Greece

Malta

Cyprus

Key

These colours are used to show where one country ends and another begins.

Europe

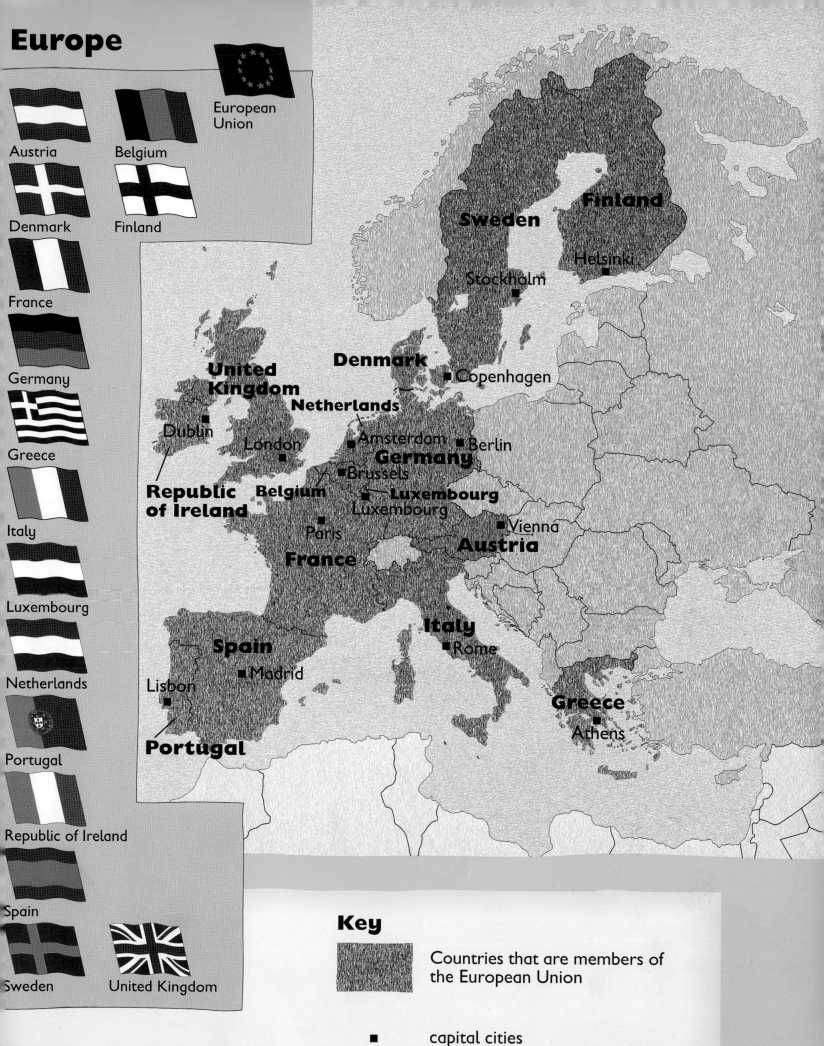

Austria

Belgium

European Union

Denmark

Finland

France

Germany

Greece

Italy

Luxembourg

Netherlands

Portugal

Republic of Ireland

Spain

Sweden

United Kingdom

Sweden

Finland

Helsinki ■

Stockholm ■

Denmark

Copenhagen ■

United Kingdom

Netherlands

Dublin ■

Amsterdam ■

Berlin ■

Germany

London ■

Brussels ■

Republic of Ireland

Belgium

Luxembourg

Luxembourg ■

Vienna ■

Paris ■

Austria

France

Italy

Rome ■

Spain

Madrid ■

Lisbon ■

Greece

Athens ■

Portugal

Key

Countries that are members of the European Union

■ capital cities

The European Union.

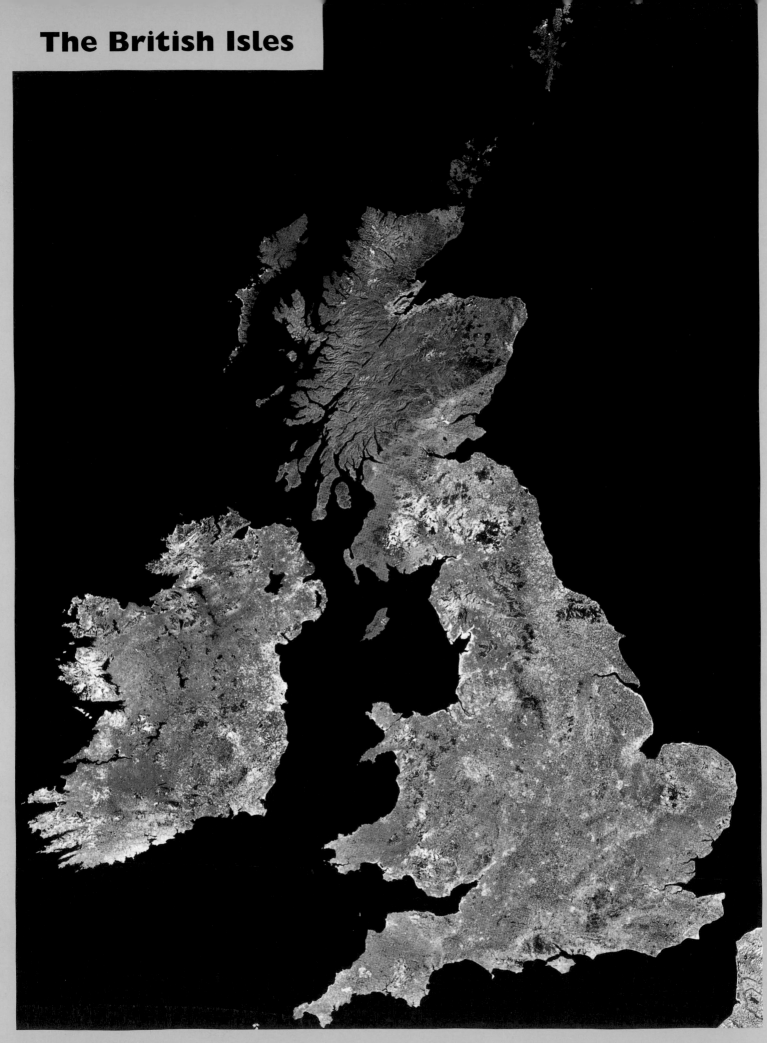

26   This is a picture from a satellite in space.

The British Isles

Key

land

sea

Shetland Islands

Orkney Islands

Lewis

Skye

Prime Meridian

North Atlantic Ocean

North Sea

Isle of Man

Irish Sea

Ireland

Anglesey

Great Britain

North Atlantic Ocean

Isle of Wight

English Channel

Scale

0   100 km

Channel Islands

There are two large islands and many small ones.

The British Isles

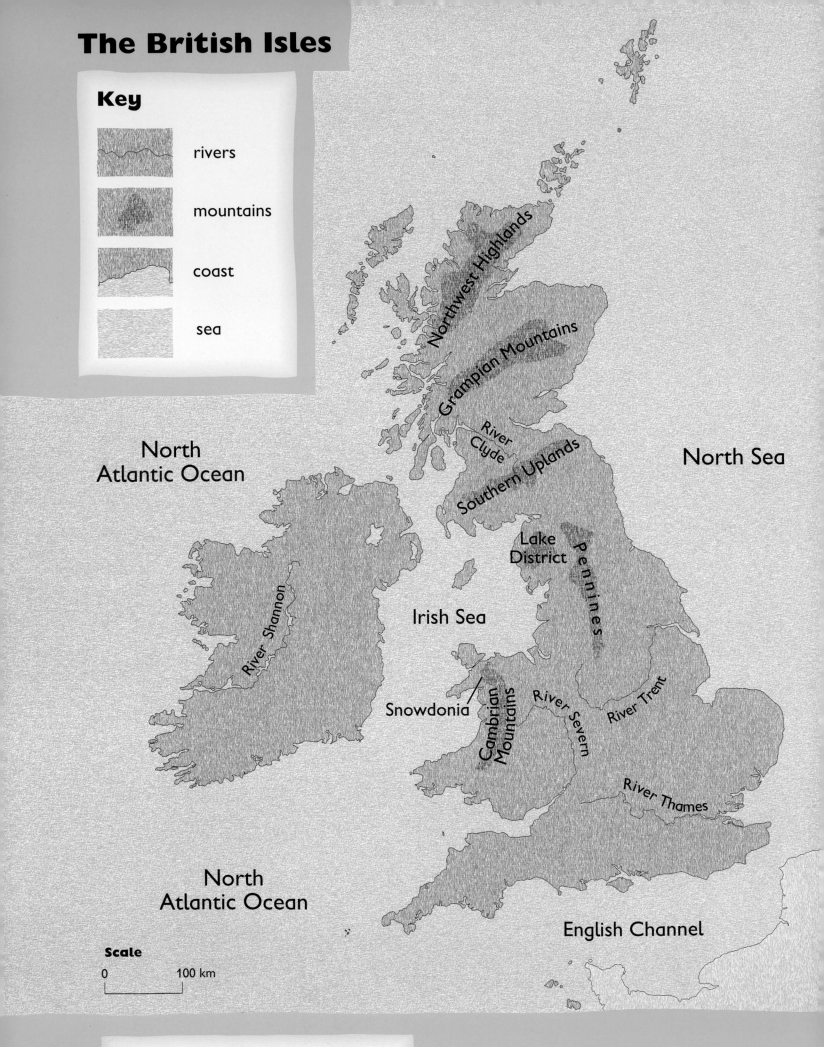

Key

rivers

mountains

coast

sea

North Atlantic Ocean

North Sea

Northwest Highlands

Grampian Mountains

River Clyde

Southern Uplands

Lake District

Pennines

Irish Sea

River Shannon

Snowdonia

Cambrian Mountains

River Severn

River Trent

River Thames

North Atlantic Ocean

English Channel

Scale

0   100 km

Rivers and mountains.

The British Isles

Key

- ■   capital cities

England, Scotland, and Wales, together with Northern Ireland, make the **United Kingdom of Great Britain and Northern Ireland.**

England   Scotland   Wales

The **Republic of Ireland** is a separate country

Scotland

United Kingdom

■ Edinburgh

Northern Ireland
■ Belfast

Republic of Ireland

■ Dublin

Isle of Man

England

Wales

Cardiff ■

London ■

Scale

0   100 km

Channel Islands

Countries and capitals.

The British Isles

Key

■ capital cities

● some other major cities

Glasgow

Edinburgh

Belfast

Newcastle upon Tyne

Dublin

Bradford ● Leeds

Liverpool ● Manchester

Sheffield

Nottingham

Leicester

Birmingham

Coventry

Cardiff

Bristol

London

Scale

0   100 km

Major cities.

The British Isles

Key

castles	
historic buildings and monuments	
theme parks	
wildlife parks and zoos	
seaside towns	

Glamis

Edinburgh

New Lanark
(Industrial Village)

Culzean

Ulster
History Park

Belfast

Dundrum

Kells
(High crosses)

Scarborough

Blackpool

Rhyl

Knowsley Safari Park

Dublin

Bunratty Castle
and Folk Park

Caernarfon

Chester

Alton Towers

Great
Yarmouth

Rock of
Cashel

Ironbridge

Warwick

Whipsnade Wild
Animal Park

Fota
Wildlife
Park

Stratford-upon-Avon
(Shakespeare's Birthplace)

Cotswold Wildlife Park

London

Thorpe Park

Tower of
London

Stonehenge

Brighton

Chessington
World of Adventures

Scale

0   100 km

Some places to visit.

Index

name of place

London   *city*   20, 25, 29, 30

what it is

the pages where you will find it

A list of the continents, countries and cities in this atlas.